LIGHTS IN THE DISTANCE

JOSEPH
CHIARI

LIGHTS
IN THE
DISTANCE

LONDON / ENITHARMON PRESS / 1971

First published in 1971 by the Enitharmon Press,
22 Huntingdon Road, East Finchley, London N2

Copyright © 1971 by Joseph Chiari

Printed and made in Great Britain

SBN 901111 24 4 (cloth)
SBN 901111 33 3 (wrappers)

TO JOY

What seas what shores what grey rocks and what islands
What water lapping the bow
And scent of pine and the woodthrush singing through the fog
What images return
O my daughter!

T.S. ELIOT: MARINA

CONTENTS

I

I

CORSICA

A landscape which breaks the heart
And a child in a world of ghosts
Trying to grasp with a wrinkled hand
A wistful star in the pale blue sky.

Scented shrubs, trees straight as rods
And among them, green years and the ache
Of receding dreams flowing back
To griefless dawns of singing woods.

Under the sun when it flails the plain
In the rage of summer, in the shade of a tree,
By the white-laced, aquamarine sea,
Or along dusty roads sizzling in the rain,

Always the same marvel of man into child,
King of the winged and leafy world,
Dancing in the glory of his newly-born days
And stabbed to the heart by the thought of spent years.

ISLAND-BORN

Island-born, sea-spawned,
The sea is the mirror
Where I learnt all I can remember;
As soon as my eyes could focus
On the horizon, I stood transfixed
By sails or smoke drawing in the sky
Paintings of unknown lands.

Later on, dazzled by magic leaves,
All ships carried Helen and Paris,
Aeneas fleeing Dido, or Columbus
Searching for his truth—the Indies,
Beyond tall steeples and cathedral waves,
To the ultimate shore of no return.
How often have I watched from my window
This feathered shape sailing westward,
Past redeeming whirls of blue flames
Towards golden sands and silence!

O my island of craggy rocks
And green-covered slopes
Lulled by the whispering sea
Which enfolds you in her arms!
What longings, what dreams
You must once have raised
In the lonely head of a fallen eagle—
Your son, pinned like an owl
To the barn door of an atlantic rock,
Waiting for death to lift him
On her wings and bring him home!

O to lie dazed on your scorching rocks,
Teased by the song of cicadas at noon,
To watch the golden locks of wheat
Sway in the breeze and the blazing sun,
Or the moon turn the proud oak
Into a god-carved silver head!
O my island, burnt out by summer heat
Drunk under the weight of fruit,
When, o when shall I see again
Your wild butterflies and shimmering light,
When shall I hear again
The organ music of your pine-trees
And when will your rosy dawn
Rub its scented nose at my window?

An air of ancestral doom hangs
Over this place, olive trees like hawks
Claw the rocky chest of the earth,
Seeking to deny the giant's strength.

Motley-skinned lizards scurry in holes
And the tingling bells of goats pierce
The veil of silence which swiftly falls
From the hills to these darkening slopes.

On either side of the road, the remains
Of a few houses, a communal oven
Strewn with shards and a derelict garden
Spell out the misdeeds of civilization.

Propt against these torn, roofless walls,
A chestnut tree preens its glistening leaves;
At its feet, a stream uncoils its limbs
Over the dark snouts of crouching rocks.

On the floor of one of these ghostly houses
The black carcass of a dead goat
Sprawls like a heraldic painting
On the walls of a primitive cave.

By its side a Greek God—Dionysos—
Sadly sings of centuries past
And slowly walks in the greying light
Towards the blue oblivion of night.

NOON-DAY SUN

The noon-day sun fills the valley
And drives birds and animals to sleep
In the brooding silence of the brushwood;
A golden hawk hangs from the blue,
Above the still, shimmering stream;
Nothing moves except the human cells
Endlessly falling towards the waiting sea,
While pinned to memory's banks, the mind
Watches with mounting sorrow
The fading light and deepening furrows.

Water flows but does not alter;
It is the same everywhere;
Flower- or snow-covered, the earth,
Indifferent whore, gives or receives
With a blank face; man alone—
A cage filled with fleeing birds—
Grieves at their loss and ever sees
Beyond spring-blossom and singing leaves,
The bed of clay which for him waits.

Heavenly music, hallowed hours
Which sometimes dispel the dark
And give tongue to singing oaks,
Cannot hide the haunting hum
Of gestating earth and sighing grass
And the rattle of bones battered by rain
Or tossed about by playing dogs.

FILITOSA

It is the end of the day; the sun
Slowly hauls his golden nets
Over tree-tops, green slopes
And the lingering gaze of glaucous pools.

Caught in the mesh of this golden trail,
A stone statue, rectangular from shoulder
To toe, stands still amid boulders,
Guarding the peace of these lonely hills.

Lengthwise sword and diagonal dagger,
Crowned by a flat, hairy head
Compose the proud bearing of the warrior
Who stands on guard over his dead;

Yonder tumulus rising behind him
Is the place where they lie buried
Or burnt, under strangely carved stones,
In the age-long rest where they were laid.

Beyond this mound, across a river,
Four knights of different size
Lined up shoulder to shoulder
Indifferent to moon—or sunrise,

Watch over the remains of their brethren—
Our ancestors who thirty thousand years ago
Squabbled, laughed, lived and died
With joys and fears which are ours also.

Dusk is falling over the wounded earth,
And from this millenary mound, whispering bones
And flowing blood ceaselessly proclaim the truth
That creation is intent upon stone.

FILITOSA is a place in the south west of Corsica, where menhirs, statues and burial mounds, dating from the Megalithic age, have recently been unearthed.

What is it that turns my thoughts
Toward you my surf-laced island
With white-headed mountain tops
And winding ribbons of glittering sand?

Why is it that before, I could only dream
Of maps, compasses and the way ahead,
Never looking back at the receding seas
Or at crying gulls flying landwards?

What mysterious voice calls me home
From dark woodlands and sea-caves,
What force ceaselessly urges me on
To retrace my steps over the waves?

Is it the slanting sun and fading light,
Is it the church bells ringing evensong,
Or have the visions which filled my mind
Fled like migrating birds in autumn?

What is home, where is home?
Is it my island with scented shrubs,
Or golden Pythagoras's uncharted isle
To which we all sail without return?

DISTANT VALLEY

The language I understand best
Is that of leaves muttering dissent
Or whispering advice and support
Whenever I need it most.

The sound that sinks deepest
In memory's pool and echoes
Down the years, back to curly locks
And bare feet on burning earth,

Is that of water leaping from stone
To stone, glistening over green scales,
Winking, whistling heavenly tunes
And filling with voices the living vale.

The dance that moves me most
Is that of pine-needles tossed by the wind
Gracefully whirling green limbs
Reflecting the light of shimmering pools.

The sight I love best is the sun
Majestically enthroned on a mountain range
Showering down its white wisdom
With prodigal, indifferent hands.

In this brimming light all stands still,
The senses fade away from the mind
Back to limpid dawns filled with birds
Calling each to each from the hills,

Until the sudden fall of a leaf
Stills the heart to stone
With the thought that all that ripens
Must fall to dark, waiting earth.

ASCO

The giant's brow broods upon its solitude
Watching, with disdain, pigmy pines
Forward bent, trying in vain to crawl
Along its furrowed chest to its forehead;

At its knees, a river roars in anger
And dances and leaps from rock to rock
To show that if it can't stand on air
It has nimble feet, speech and no roots.

Mountains are tied by the waist to the earth
Trees are held down by giant hands
And they shake in vain their angry heads
As powerless as Samson at Delilah's feet.

Water mocks them both with its foam
Its headlong tumbles and varied songs
Its merry-go-round across lands and oceans
Which will last the whole earth-long.

On its banks, man, untied the while,
Yet earth-bound—a seeming of presence,
A metaphor caught in falls and pools—
Longs for roots and the death of conscience.

ASCO *is one of the most striking inland valleys of Corsica.*

The water, liquid diamond, leaps
From stone to stone; on its bank, marigolds
Spill their scent over a motley mosaic,
Reflecting the changing schemes of light.

A lark, aloft in the blue,
Pours down the gratuity of its joy
On the lap of carefree mother nature—
Closed womb of earth and sky.

Light flows down from indifferent heaven,
Water follows the laws of its density,
And a clump of trees set in green
Composes a picture of pre-human serenity;

Alone, the remains of a fire stain the sand
Disclosing the incinerated human fact;
No other self but my own intrudes
Upon the plenitude of non-being.

With it, the worm in the fruit—
Man — maker of meaning and death,
Stills the song in the lark's throat
And turns water to tears and music to sighs.

What remains? A broken mirror,
A collage-picture made to tell
A tale gratuitously imposed upon nature
By man ever intent on having his will!

SPIDERS

A spider propels itself in space
Slowly sliding up to the green lobes
Of chestnut leaves, the palace
Where it weaves its princely robes;

Another descends the ladder of heaven,
A small brown patch, swinging
On nothing, till it alights on the green
Spire of a cathedral pine.

Far away, in the distance, the red eye
Of the sun enfolds in its glowing gaze
The silvery limbs of a birch tree
Shaking its locks in a hush of gold.

I sit still, watching sun and sky
Conjure up sleep upon the earth,
And caught in unease, I wonder why
I too could not walk on air,

I wonder what keeps me earthbound!
Is it the weight of matter, the lack
Of a solid, yet unbreakable thread,
Or the wings which lifted Jacob?

I wonder why a spider knows
Its way to heaven, and I don't;
I wonder what is the *I* that dreams
And the flesh that ties it to earth,

I wonder and keep on wondering
While the blue, thickening air
Slowly hushes all whisperings
And stills the leaves to a shudder,

Until all dreams and longings sink
Into a metaphysic of silence,
And the lengthening shadow of trees
And a faint haze soon close the book,

Leaving all questions unanswered.

Night falls, the light recedes
Over the sinuous sea;
The moon rises, trailing its red
Gauze over the orange-fringed waves,
The owl stands still in the oak-tree
Waiting to be sure that his enemy—
The sun—is safely asleep in his cave.

Soon, the croaking of frogs in watery leaves
Sweeps out of the sky all human cries;
All things fade, and turn into shades
Slow-rising sap and haunted silence.

Only the moon remains,
Tired bald pate,
Hollow, blind eye,
Wandering mournfully
Across the plains
Of the sky.

NAPOLEON'S STATUE AT LAFFREY, 11 PM

Glistening like steel in a ghostly light
Horseman and Horse surge from the ground
Forefeet raised as if to take flight
And leap straight out of the world.

II

Sometimes, wandering in the dark
Along luminous paths
Known to you alone,
Spelling incantations to the wind
And probing the silence of stones,
You ask why life's comedy
Should be so strangely staged
And criss-crossed with paradoxes
That only death can solve them.

Far away, on the other side of being,
Caught in the craters of the moon,
Longing for the absent sun,
I hear your anxious questioning
But cannot give you an answer;

Like a sleeper in a nightmare,
I see it all, the joys lost,
The rise and fall of seasons,
The hot summer and recurring frost,
The falling dark and burnt-out dawns,
Yet can do nothing but shout
In silence and strive in paralysis,
Until we have found our true meaning
On the same side of being.

Wouldn't you like to tear mountains apart
And reach the vale of unquenched fires
Or heave the hawsers and let the boat
Ride the waves towards obsessing horizons!

Wouldn't you like to shake off ties and trees,
To shut off your ears to sounds and calls
And wildly plunge into the rising seas
To be rolled away to unknown landfalls!

Wouldn't you like the hush of a desert wind
Across your face, drying up your tears,
Burning your thoughts, scorching your limbs
With astral music to drown all fears!

You need not answer! your eyes unfold
The ebb and flow of brooding storms,
Your hands carve worlds on air;
And your lips quiver in aching prayer.

Yet in the dark of your head, a light
Flickers like a beam over rough seas
And warns you of shipwrecks and the night
Which its fading out would let loose,

So, with your heart in your hands
You stumble on through mounting shadows
Your limbs flailed by burning winds
Caught in the tides of unredeemed sorrow.

I cannot compare you to this or that,
Make a cosmic map out of your shape,
And sing the discovery of its hills and coves
As if I were Columbus or a modern astronaut;

I cannot; actions need no words,
And words and thoughts are private
And cannot be used to construct
Exhibits for others to deny or applaud.

Our love is its own infinite end
Excluding listeners or sight-seers;
The world only needs to know, if it cares,
That you can turn darkness into light,

That like a river intent upon the ocean
Your clear waters knowing no marshlands
Or weed-ridden banks, move forward
Life-giving, reflecting heaven,

That like some Greek statues, you've no hands
To take from others; only a centre filled
With golden substance, freely offered
To transfigure all—this world, and beyond.

When night falls upon my eyes
And folds away for time's length
My aimless arms still intent
Upon the shadow of your shape,

Then my mind will ache no more
Nor dread the years waned away
Waiting in vain for your return
And the harvest gold of autumn,

Then stillness will heal all wounds,
And whatever form you take,
Whether you live in a star
Or join the endless fall of black suns,

I shall know you, when stone you roll
By my side, or rain you fall
On the grass where I shall lie
Listening for sounds of known sighs.

If you live on leaves or wings,
I shall be the wind of the solar seas
Bringing to you, memories of spring
And songs from earthly skies,

Trees will rustle with your voice
Weeping grass will shed your tears
Water will echo the sound of your steps,
And every line compose your face,

Then fear shall be no more,
For freed from eyes and hands
I shall find and see you everywhere,
And nameless we shall live
Beyond Time and melting sands.

Try as I may I can never replace
With words or works your absent face,
Walking the streets, watching falling leaves,
Following dreams on the wings of birds,
Or listening to sparrows squabbling on eaves,
I can never succeed in exorcising the ghost
Whose footsteps echo in my heart,
Or forget the silence of your voice.

All things partake of you, and while I converse
With you, the words take your place,
Become you, and I become you also,
King of endless moments, oblivious
Of harrowing Time and gnawing winds,
Until a stone slips from under my foot,
And I stumble once more into a dark hole,
Face to face with my naked self.

You must have gone away with the Pliocene night!
And after your departure, the great ice age
Suddenly covered the earth, and light
Stumbled and turned all things into your image.
Dinosaurs and mammoths, cumbersome as I am,
Caught in unwisdom, unable to follow the winds
Which wafted you away to palmy shores,
Remained trapped like fleas under a helmet,
Or grass under ice, waiting for the sun to rise,
Or a tilt of the earth for release.

So, millions of years have passed,
Oceans have swayed to and fro across the earth,
Squandering on rocks their lace and diamonds,
Mountains have risen and fallen,
And forked animals have moved from caves to plains,
Picking up grain, pecked by wind and rains,
Learning to replace silex and bone with iron,
And thus to become the scourge of the earth.

And all this time, while you were away
Rocks were loosened, the earth's skin was torn open,
Quicksands and rolling mud became tombs,
And I have seen cities and empires come and go
Frontiers sway to and fro, and killing with stone,
At close quarters, turn into killing from heaven!
I have seen Caesar cower in despair, and Christ
And his twelve apostles build a cathedral of fishes

And sow the seeds of life by the Galilean shores.
And great, bitter winds have swept the earth,
Wars, revolutions, plagues, have invaded
A blind world, adrift on the verge of the void;
And during all this time, you were away,
I don't know where, in some distant sun
Whose rays will, one day, shatter the doors of darkness,
And its wild music overwhelm the drums of silence.

Thus the earth which will receive you
Is already torn open by Time's plough
And the ice which will enfold you
Is creeping along the walls of your cells.

Unseen by you moves the black banner
Which sweeps over trees and stones
And turns the green and gold of summer
Into the grey ashes of unborn dawns.

A silent fire is consuming your days
Until you are nothing but smouldering embers—
A seeming of living, which black wings
Brushing past, will disperse to the winds.

All that we are is the result of our thoughts,
Said the Buddha under his Bo-tree,
Yet, in spite of that, all Penelope's efforts
Could not wean Ulysses from the rival sea.

What are thoughts which cannot turn to deeds?
A piercing flame, a gnawing pain
A rending claw and grinding wind
Causing deeper furrows than sea or rain.

III

Grief in art must be cleansed
From the tensions and sorrows of the heart;
Its component parts must be hauled
Out of the sea of memory and fused
By the cool, flameless fire of the mind
Which lives in a world of its own
Free from tears, thoughts and emotions.

Grief must surge from uncharted depths,
Winged up by the urge to light,
Towards imagined, living shapes—
Timeless incandescences of foam
On the ever-changing ocean of Time;

Grief is not personal, it comes from Adam
—God's tear on the hot crust of the earth
Where the liquid sky mirrored his solitude
Until Eve turned the mirror into a dark wood,

And ever since, the progeny of Abel and Cain
And the animals which Time has bred
Have blundered on, carrying in their hearts
The original grief of Adam's pain—

That of being born, and of knowing
That men can only think of grief
By going back to the first falling leaf
Which shook Adam from his green sleep.

WHY IS IT?

Why is it, as Baudelaire said,
That the heart-beats and changing pulse
To which a haunting landscape gives rise
Are always stilled by the thought of death?

While, whether we soar with Rembrandt's *Night Watch,*
Christ's agony in his *Descent from the Cross,*
Or St Jerome's musings by his grinning skull,
Nothing disturbs these self-begotten flights.

Earth's beauty is the living *I*
Conscious of being and of dying;
Art's beauty is timeless,
It does not create, it dispels fear,

It shows that the dark can be set alight
And that mortal man can turn
Consuming fires into golden forms
Which will illumine for ever his earthly path.

What else makes man but his gaiety
Which levels black with white,
Enables him to ride the surf of sorrows
And accept the approach of falling night?

What's the use of shouting against the roar
Of the ocean or moaning against the wind
Which sweeps on from distant shores
And grinds all fears in the mill of the mind?

Nothing can be altered by our cries,
The great Deities will not bend their heads
And the wide-eyed birds which ply the sky
Will not be halted in their wild races,

The tides will not cease to sieve
In their to-and-fro the pebbles of the shore,
The trees will shed no leaves
And the dead will not break their slumber,

Nothing that man does can stop
The sad song of the chained sea
Which raves and rails with its waves
At the immobility of the imprisoning rocks.

THE SNOWMAN

The snowman in the garden
Which yesterday was six feet tall
Is today down to ground level
And about to fade under the earth.

Time and the sun have shrunk him
To the shape which will sleep
In the loam, or ceaselessly ride
The transparent horses of the moon.

Like snow in the sun, the blood
Thickens and passes from gold to lead
Which suddenly stiffens the knees
And removes the rider from his horse,

And the silent, shadow race continues;
Unshod, unbridled, tireless horses
Gallop across the fields of the earth,
Led by the undying horseman—Death!

A mangy dog paws the air
Rubbing his back on the grass
To shake a flea or allay an itch;
An old woman shudders on a bench,
A blackbird sways back and forth
Hauling up an unwilling worm,
While green leaves wave you by
On your indifferent road.

You are being followed, wherever you go;
When you sleep, she lies by your side
Until the fateful dawn
When she will rise and leave you behind;
When you walk, she sidles by you
More faithful than your shadow
Until the day when she will loosen
Your knees or cut your sinews,
And you will drop to the ground.

A dog feels his fleas and his needs
But does not know that he is followed;
A beetle blunders across your path
Unmindful of your death-carrying foot;
Man alone nurses this shadow
In his heart and this light in his skull.

Prospero's magic was of no avail to him,
Every third thought became his grave
Until his thought and his grave were one.

O to seize the flowing fountain and to freeze
Its stream in an ever-present moment,
To uproot the pine tree and to transplant
It in the palm of the hand or the forehead,
To hold time like a spinning top
Stilled for ever in front of the eyes!

O the aching dream of spent hours!
Yet, which one would one choose
To live over and over again till the end
And how could the choice be reduced to one?
What could sum up such a dream
Which heavenly music, which vision?

These very words take one out of time
And show that the transfixed moment
Which the mind wants to hold forever
Is not a fact but the vision of a fact,
For the greatest joy-giving event
Endlessly repeated would become hell,
The fountain would pierce the head
The tree force its roots through the heart
The entrancing voice would turn to a howl,
And the sweet, heart-rending lips
Would be as harrowing as Satan's fire.

The world's weight may lie still
In the palm of the hand; the winds
May drop, the sails
Slacken, but not the questing mind.

On and on it goes, asking why we are here,
What purpose we are meant to fulfill
And what sorrow or shame we must endure
Before we reach the other side of the hill.

Wherever we turn, to lofty mountains,
Plains, lakes, rolling waters
Or voices long-stilled under stone,
We always get the same answer;

Christ got his own upon the cross,
Our fast-decaying flesh unfolds
The scroll where at the end it lies,
To be finally read with closed eyes;

We move from far away, beyond blood,
Bones, wombs or friendly smiles,
Out of a merry dance of molecules
Into the weightless sleep of the infinite.

Not the years but death alone
Can still the senses of the poet,
And there lie the salt of regret
And the source of sighs and moans.

How sad when caught in the wind
Of spring, the sails suddenly fall
Leaving the boat stone-still
Longing for the wide, rolling horizon!

How lovingly the trees bend their heads
And stretch their branches and leaves
Over this swiftly passing shadow
Haunted by the light of summer eves!

O the rage of a wild bird
Longing for seas and high mountains
Locked in a cage of fragile bones
With a more and more rarefied air!

Its eyes still go on scanning the horizon
Continuously drawing across the sky
The elemental geometry of its origins—
The shortest line between prey and eye;

But now, it's all eyes and no prey
The iron bars have come closer
The roof's rafters are lower
And the horizon looms grey, like clay.

What makes a man walk on
With steady steps towards the hilltop
Where dazzling light will darken his gaze
And dissolve him in the enfolding night?

What song, what music or faith
Can drown his fears and growing sorrows
In a world of pendent branches
Thinning woods and dried-up river beds?

Hope, fear of eternal punishment,
Fear of infinite silence and darkness,
Fear of unknown, uncharted seas
With tempests greater than he knows!

Perhaps! But fear never fed the heart
Or hauled saints over rocks and sands
Clasping the future in their cupped hands,
Unmindful of thorns and tattered flesh;

Only fire can dispel all fears
And keep at bay crouching beasts
Beckoning shadows and anguished thoughts,
Till light descends and redeems the desert.

What else is there for man to think about
Except the fast-fading sands
And the unfailing, rising roar
Of the dark, all-embracing sea?

Whenever the mind disconnects from the senses
Or turns its gaze from the patch where it grazes
All he sees is memories tossed like leaves
In the wind, and dark wings
Brushing past, hovering over him
Hurrying him to the dark entrance
And the dissolving, subterranean waves
Which Eurydice sought in vain to leave.

Now that the stars which crowded the sky
Have mostly sunk beyond the horizon
Now that I no longer ride the horses of the blue
Looking for the rising wings of infinite joys,

Now that desire and dreams have ceased
To confuse my sight and blur my mind,
I can concentrate on the white-maned waves
And hear beyond the gulls' cry the roar of the land.

No more gazing into the blue of the sky
Or into the blue, grey or green of eyes,
No more dreaming of the music of the spheres
Of journeys, mountains and lost princesses.

The island is in sight, and one single stride
Could take me into paradise, or into nothingness,
Where the loom of Eternity will consume
The wronged flesh, and music and light
Restore the equilibrium of the heart and mind
To the essential fluid which feeds all cells
And ties the wandering earth to the eye of the Sun.

SLANTING SUN

Trees full of shapes,
Earth full of sounds,
Blue sky—gauze on skin
And across haunting eyes;
Why this music, these colours
And these all-embracing gossamers!

Whom do they want to delay
enchant or imprison,
In this dying, slanting sun
Pouring its golden sadness
Over the green shawls of trees
And the brooding silent stones?

Yet, do they really care?
Is not this the anguished cry
Of the heart stabbed with sorrow
At the perennial joy of trees,
The miracle-less face of mountains
And the whispers of waiting stones!

And soon, trees show their bare bones,
Crystal streams turn soggy brown,
Rocks take the shape of mausoleums
And the light fades in a widening grin.

In spring, trees like youth
Have only one concern—
To move as far as possible from their roots
And to caparison themselves in green.

Head high in search of light
They stretch out their limbs and stalk about
Toppling one another in delight,
Indifferent to what crawls on the ground.

In autumn, with all lust spent
And leaves like golden coins around them,
Trees have tongues and tears to commune
With the mind-ridden glow-worms at their feet.

Their pride has gone and they know the pain
And the pull of the roots, and they wonder—
Cruellest question of all—how long it will be
Before they are out of sun and wind
And can only hear the trickle of the rain.

A WALK IN THE PARK

Cerulean blue strewn with white scarves
Tossed by the wind; autumn colours—
Russet and green and falling leaves—
The nearby pond shimmers in the sun.

The earth exudes heat after the storm
And out of the haze, two penguin nuns
Step out in time, towards Heaven
Which nods at them right above the green.

A thrush baptises himself in the joy
Of a puddle; head down, tail up,
The world is a splash of diamonds
And a reel round the axle of his bill.

In this scene, man, outsider and recorder,
Ignored by all, yet holding all in his mind
Wonders how long it will be before painter
And picture are one and the same thing.

THE SHADOW

From the moment when dawn broke
Upon my face, your shadow, dark,
Hollow-eyed, age-worn, rose in my wake
And has followed me night and day.

As the swelling and shrinking moon
Follows the sun, you've followed me,
Known all my joys and all my dreams
And slept by my side in my every bed.

With you I have roamed the world;
I have tried to lose you, ignore you
Or to drown you in insults or oblivion,
But all my attempts have been in vain.

If I shut my eyes so as not to see you
You lift the roof of my head and come in
And if I turn right or left to avoid you,
I always find your dark shape in my arms.

Who are you and what is your name,
Above all what do you want,
Why do you follow me, and what port,
Will you, at last, let me enter alone?

—I am your double, I am the raging breath
Which flamed you out of the dark
For a brief dream between womb
And grave, and my name is Death.

I have been, and will always be with you
Every moment of your heart's beats,
And I shall only cease to follow you
When, enfolded under my rising wings,
And in luminous dark and silence,
You and I are reflected by the same eye.

Scientists in their laboratories,
Astronomers in their cool chambers,
All, wholly aseptic, dressed in white,
Inoculated against emotions and passions,
Washed clean from desires and volitions,
Masked, gloved, glass-caged,
Observe unmoved the faked pregnancies
Of the moon, the red tails of quasars,
And record, without a flutter in their pulse,
Facts, figures, concepts, hypotheses,
Called pure, immaculate knowledge,
In contrast with the emotion-soiled,
Bowel-stained knowledge of the poet and the sage.

Archimedes had only to lounge in his bath
To tumble to the truth that the bigger the rump
The stronger the push towards the light
—A strange contradiction between matter and spirit,
But Seneca had to use his bath to cut his veins
So as to teach the world the meaning of ingratitude,
And Socrates had to drain the bitter cup
To assert the wisdom of unwisely applied laws.

Newton cast a cold eye on a falling apple,
And deduced from it the law of gravitation;
And Dante had to be snubbed at the church door
And made to eat the bitter bread of exile,
Before he could wring from his Aeolian heart
The great song of the human condition.

The sun breathes and moves over the sea,
Which swells with desire, shudders
In all her cells, glistens, and heaves
Her countless bosoms towards his thirst
And the burning embrace from which truth
And illumination are endlessly born.

The Sun and the Sea are for ever locked
In a tangled rhythm of rises and falls,
Of wild music, high flood tides,
And bridal sleep in the shadow of the Moon.

The Sea unfolds her vast, fecund depths,
To the kiss of light and the pull of the heights,
And the two, rolled in the same wave, create life
And the divine truth which never divides,
But always unites, and never allows the separation
Of the Music, or of the Dancer, from the Dance.

WHY?

Why this ceaseless piling up of words
Upon words—Pelion upon Ossa,
Sisyphus's endless trek! To what end,
Above all, what causes this fever?

What world am I trying to reach
Or to forget, or, is it both in one!
Am I trying to achieve forgetfulness
Or protest against darkling oblivion?

Why write, why paint, if not to kill
Time and dredge up the truth
From deep down the dark well
Whence we came and to which we return?

Why this itch which only ink can cool,
Why this urge to pin upon walls
The butterflies of the mind, or pour out
On white the hidden streams of the heart!

Rabbits would die if they couldn't file
Their teeth against the trees' bark and roots,
Writers would choke or burst like fruit
If they couldn't let out the lava of their minds.

Why is it so? Why do salmon return
To the waters of their birth, why do tigers
Kill, or glow-worms shine in the dark!
It's all part of the same mysterious order.

We are born and we have to die,
Whatever we may do; every autumn
Leaves turn to gold, and winter
Follows, and they moulder in the snow.

New leaves will grow, new men
Will be born, but that's no consolation
For what sleeps in the earth and never returns
Or lives, except in the mind of those who live on.

Is the pain we feel at falling leaves
The dark premonition of the dreaded fall
From the white-walled cities of life,
Through fold upon fold of primal shadows?

Perhaps, perhaps, for it is hard
To leave this world and face alone
The long sea-journey which divides
The old from the new, the known from the unknown.

Is art man's cry against Death,
Are the phosphorescent temples of the mind
The silvery lights which defy the dark
And, bodyless, linger in the wake of the earth!

In their caves, thousands of years ago,
Men pinned their dreams on rocks
And with them, denied space and the dark
And broke the fetters of fear and sorrows.

Since then, irrespective of climes, men
Have continued to cage haunting beasts
In the meshes of mind and imagination
So as to keep at bay the crowding night.

THE SADNESS OF GOD

High above the burnt-out Earth,
On the threshold of the sun, sorrow-struck,
With furrowed brow and pierced heart,
Tears flowing down the light of His cheeks,
Forlorn Father in Pietà, sits God.

His liquid gaze sweeping over the face
Of Chronos-Earth sees nothing but ghosts
And mangled heaps of flesh, caught
In the flames of man's daemonic fires
And turned to charred, black shapes.

After millions of years during which sun,
Rain, wind and snowfalls
Had fed flowers, animals and seas
From which God's fallen star—Man—
Arose and grew among the green,

The Earth has turned to black; leaves
And trees are withered; the seas
Roll in their waves the black carcases
Of dead fish, and the Earth's surface
Is strewn with accusing feathers and pelts.

Man has put all under Death's dominion,
Girls in their dreams, boys in their games,
Mothers, fathers, lovers, all gone,
All dispelled by man's poisoned mind,
Who first killed God and then killed himself.

And under the glare of Heaven's light,
Alone, in cyclonic silence, God weeps,
And the lava of His tears rolls down hands
Which have sought in vain to hold creation
Within the circles of His infinite Being.

How cruel and sad the sadness of God!
Who will comfort Him for His loss,
Which Angel will dare to move
Across the nothingness of the Earth's grave
And to whisper that Hope might be born again!

IN MEMORIAM J. F. KENNEDY

The eyes of men are fixed on the horizon,
Straining to hold back the fading light
Which sought to heal inhuman divisions
And to enfold East and West in one beam;

Now this light has set among constellations
Which are what they will always be
And will keep on pouring across the centuries
The wisdom and inspiration which guide all men.

If ever the muted spirit of the earth, aghast
At the roar of its own suicidal rage,
Stirred by the abyss which gapes at its feet,
Could summon again the vision of the burning bush,

And with cleansing flames consume the crust
Of fear and hunt out of men's hearts
The writhing serpents of human distrust,
It is at this hour that it would do it!

Never has there been a man more mourned,
Never have more sighs, hymns and sorrows
Risen towards the green, undefinable fields,
Where his great soul now unquietly moves;

Lured by Eternity, obsessed by the urge
To repel death, he has outdistanced it,
And has left behind the crystal of his heart,
Which will ever shine beyond loam and the ages.

You would not like me to mount a rostrum
And proclaim your virtues and greatness;
Your gentle smile and wry wisdom
Would soon dispel such inflation.

You wouldn't like me to strike up attitudes,
To parade sorrow as a dark mirror
Reflecting your great, spent light,
Or use your loss to write dull odes.

All you might allow me to say, under protest,
Is that you, who were so cool and controlled
In your verse and in the web of your thought
So perfectly master of the flow of your emotions,

Were also the most affectionate of men
The most kind-hearted of friends—
A man whose humility and capacity to love
Echoed the music of the Sermon on the Mount.

THOUGHTS BY T. S. ELIOT'S GRAVE

In my beginning is my end—that's certainty,
In my end is my beginning—there is doubt,
Except for those who stand on rock,
Like you, or the prisoner of Fotheringay.

For, this dark beginning is so different
From what we can think or know
That even those enfolded in Christ's arms
Tremble at the thought of the light
Which will blot out their senses
And wrench them out of their roots
Like whirling leaves in roaring winds.

Even if they long in their hearts for the comfort
Of seeing without eyes, or if they believe
That what they will see in the colourless world
Will transform them into eternal song,
How can the mind, how can the heart
Forsake without terror the scent of flowers
The tides of the senses and the music of colours?
The dear friend on whose tombstone
I knelt today had no such doubts;
Neither had Pascal, yet, infinite space
Frightened him, infinitely small,
Simply because the loss of identity
The disintegration of the cells, frighten us all.

Christ in us, Christ around us,
Ever present, through life without end,
Strengthens us, comforts us, yet the cry
Which came to His lips in the half-lit garden
Comes also to ours in our bitter hour
Which tears apart the music from the shell,
For the shell is also the music,
And we cannot bear the thought of being
Nothing but music in celestial spheres.

All attempts at consolation, all words
Are barren, fruitless, full of dust,
Every human explanation makes it worse,
Is less than useless, for it destroys
The nothingness of light and the music
In which, mindless, senseless, we truly are,
Without knowing who we are.

The picture of Christ as King, Leader
Of hosts, as warrior of holy causes,
Deprives me of Christ, because these clothes
Diminish and darken the great light
Which holds together kings and beggars,
Warriors and non-warriors, vanquished and victors.
Christ is infinite silence; His name
Endlessly repeated is the best music;
Christ is dazzling darkness, light
Of life and death; His coming to earth,
His death on earth were His wisdom
And purpose, and no one can be praised
Because He chose to be born a Jew,
Just as no one can be blamed
Because He chose to die among them,
For it was a God-chosen death,
And He gave Judas the kiss of peace.

Are these thoughts heretical,
Which came to me, dear friend,
As I was kneeling in prayer,
Thinking of you, certain that if a spirit
Had refined itself into the readiness for God,
Had striven to shed its impurities
And to live by love and Christ's teaching,
It was yours!

O shall I ever pierce the secret
Of that innocent, silent stare,
When huddled up in crumpled sheets,
Your breath hovering on the edge of sleep,
Your blood suspended between water and stone,
Your shrunken body burnt into a living soul,
You looked and looked and with aching hands
Tried to utter words or thoughts welling
Up from the depths towards which you were falling!

What cold hand did you feel,
What wild light did you see
Which your silent tongue
Sought in vain to reveal?

O, how sad to watch your great spirit
Struggle against the closing gates
Of the frost-laden February night
And the gaping earth waiting for you!

And while Time had melted away the years
And reduced you to the innocence of the womb,
Once again a child in the cradle
Preparing for your last birth,
We watched you behind an armoury of lies,
Encouraging you to make plans
Which we knew would be still-born,
And every night when we left you alone
The prey of the dark closing upon you
We walked away in shame and guilt
At being unable to help you.

And now that the earth is lying upon you,
By night or by day, on mountains
In forests or at sea, in aching spring
Or numbing winter, in dead silence,
Blinding rain or roaring winds,
I shall always hear your anguished whisper
And see everywhere your hurt stare.

400 copies of this book have been printed
by the Daedalus Press, Stoke Ferry, Norfolk
for the Enitharmon Press;
of these 50 are on special paper, numbered 1-50,
and signed by the author.